Fighting To Be What God Has Longed For Me To Be

Fighting For What's Right When Everything Feels Wrong

Johnelle Johnson

Dedication

I dedicate this book to my critics. I'm not trying to be cliché or anything, but they deserve this moment. Not everyone had faith in me when I told them about this book. On a constant basis I had to deal with people's negative responses about my book. I could have let the comments discourage me, but I chose to turn it into something positive and motivational. Without the critics I would not have had the drive to accomplish this book. For all the snickering and smirks, and the smart remarks, I thank you. To all the people talking behind my back and saying I was a joke, it made me grow more in my faith. I know my steps are ordered by the Lord, so even if a person does not agree with the way God is using me that is fine.

Acknowledgements

I would like to thank everyone who played a role and helped me in this process of writing this book. To begin with I would like to thank my parents. Even though they did not know about my book until the last minute, they are my parents and they raised me well. When I told them I was writing a book they made sure they informed everyone about my book.

I would like to thank my sisters Angie and Nae Nae, they learned about my book last minute as well, but they made sure they spread the word about the book and they kept me motivated as well.

My brother in law Wood played a major role in the process of writing my book. He helped me with various tasks to make sure I was well taken care of. He helped with many of the things needed to promote the book, from my flyers, photo shoot, and getting my book into the right hands.

My nephews Robert, Qwenta', and Jermaine (and my niece Trinae) helped me as well. I called them my little assistants because I needed help with a lot of small things that I could not do alone.

My friends Cetra and Christian. They listened to all of my ideas, helped me with the some story lines, and gave me a different perspective on things.

I want to thank my Pastor, Apostle Marvin Smith. He did not have anything to do with helping me with this book but he taught me well. His teaching helped me grow and made me more knowledgeable in many areas.

Elder Jamara Smith, I appreciate the fact that you were proud of me and offered to help me with coordinating a location for my release event.

Thanks to all my aunts, uncles, cousins, I love you all. And to anyone I may have forgotten to mention thank you. Much love to everyone, I'm forever grateful.

Finally, I would like to thank God for this opportunity. God could have used anybody, but he used me for this task. I was obedient to God and I was a willing vessel. This had nothing to do with me but everything to do with him.

Table of Contents

Chapter Twenty-Three

Chapter Twenty-Four

Introduction

Writing this book has to be one of the most challenging things I have ever done. I did not know how I would even go about writing this book. I did not even know where I was going to go to get the resources needed for this book. But, one thing I learned during this time is that God will make a way out of no way, and if he wants something to be done for his glorification it will happen. I came to a point while writing this book where I just stopped writing. I got so discouraged, and I think that was the devil's way of distracting me. I found myself giving the book extra deadlines, that I really did not need, I became lazy.

Then I started to think about who will read my book. What if everyone says they do not want to take any advice from a 24 year old, what does she know? I began to beat myself up because I thought I was not qualified for the task. What if everyone already knows what I am sharing? What if I say the wrong thing? Or what if I offend someone? Fear was taking over me and that is the very thing that the devil wanted.

It is not my business to worry about if someone likes or agrees with the information God gave to me to share. The only thing I should worry about is being obedient to God and he will work everything else out. Another issue that I came across was the length of my book. When I finally completed the rough draft copy I probably had about 50 pages total and I thought, "That is not a book." On a consistent basis I found myself comparing my book to other Christian books. I wanted to be taken seriously when it came to my book, so I made sure I looked everywhere possible for a sense of direction. Looking at other books I had to keep in mind that I should not go overboard or look at this book as some type of competition because it is not. I also had to keep reminding myself that I need to be content with God have given me. Whether its twenty, fifty, or two hundred pages, it is my job to work what God has given me. I am not out here trying to impress anybody but God, and if he approves of my work then that is all that matters.

I want to be like David was in the bible. He was a man after God's heart, and even though he messed up time after time he never denied God's place in his life. David wanted God's house to be just as beautiful as his house. He did not feel right knowing that his house was in order but God's was not. He wanted to be a blessing, so that is why David was so adamant about building the temple. That is how I feel about young people. I know

God wants the best for them, and their vision may be a little clouded right now, but with my ideas and the help of God we can be some planet shakers.

My goal for this book is to catch the attention of the current youth generation. The youth are in need more than ever before. And I know I may not have all the answers, but I am sure I can help someone. I like to consider myself as a unique type of Christian. Now, do not get me wrong I live according to the bible. I do not make up my own rules or anything of that nature, but I am mainly talking about how I carry myself and my outward appearance. To begin with I am "tatted up," I talk in a way where my peers can understand and relate to me (mainly slang), and the way I dress fits this generation. Some people want to define holiness by their clothing, but Jesus looked the same as his generation.

When the Roman soldiers came to get him they did not know which one he was. They found out when Judas kissed him. Now, I am not trying to justify my actions or anything, but I know what these kids are thinking because I used to be the same way, "Here goes miss goody trying to preach to us about God and she is nothing like us." My friends and I always discuss how we are so different, but because of the fact that we are so different we are going to be used as an agent for change, and we will do it in a drastic way that the church won't be able to do anything but respect us. The Bible says that in the last days "God … will pour out my spirit upon [his] people. Your sons and daughters will prophesy. Your

13

young men will see visions, and your old men will dream dreams." I have a connection with this generation, I feel for this generation, because I am this generation.

I have a couple of scriptures that speak to this connection. The first is 1 Corinthians 9:22 (NIV) where Paul says, "When I am with those who are weak, I share their weakness, for I want to bring the weak to Christ. Yes, I try to find common ground with everyone, doing everything I can to save some." If that were not enough for you what about this one which is my favorite located in 1 Corinthians 9:19-21 (NLT), "Even though I am a free man with no master, I have become a slave to all people to bring many to Christ? When I was with the Jews, I lived like a Jew to bring Jews to Christ. When I was with those who follow the Jewish Law, I too live under that law. Even though I am not subject to."

One thing that I learned while trying to live right is that we want someone who can relate to us. We do not want anyone telling us how we should live if they cannot even understand the shoes we walked in. Why do you think preachers that come from the street are well respected by young hood guys? People have more respect for a person that has common interest and common struggles. I feel as if I can be the voice of the younger generation because I understand what it is like growing up in this day and time. I grew up in the church and I know and respect everything that I learned. And yet, as I grew up I begin to see different sides of myself and the youth in church. As youth are forced to go to church we began seeing what we do not like about going to church, whether it is getting up early, the dress code, or just the attitude of Christians being judgmental.

As the youth in the church grow up we find several reasons why church is not fully for us anymore (I am not talking about your kids, I know you raised angels). I want to bring back to the youth that it is possible to be young, cool, and saved. We should not let a couple of bad experiences cloud our vision of church and the body of Christ. There is already enough temptation and battling we have to deal with while growing up and we should feel at home in the church, not like strangers. I just want to be a helping hand so the youth of this generation can understand what is at stake, which is our eternity.

Chapter One

Being Humble

Everyone cannot handle humility but most people want it. I was put in a situation where I had to be humble. My air conditioner in the house broke at the beginning of the summer, so you know it was hot! Whenever I had a problem I always found a quick solution for solving it, no matter what it was. But, in this case I couldn't solve the problem as quickly as I usually did. I decided to take out a student loan from my school to get the AC fixed and the problem would be solved. As Christians we always are looking for microwave results. Quick and easy! I was forced to wait two weeks for the loan to get processed, and IF they approve it, it will take a couple of days before I could get it. To get our AC fixed it was not just a couple of hundred dollars, it was more like two thousand dollars. Now two thousand dollars may not be a lot of money to some people, but for a working middle class family it is a lot. I see my family struggle on a constant day-to-day basis and I knew it would not be much stress for me if I was to take care of the problem. For some reason every loan I applied for I could not get because I needed to be enrolled in summer classes. I went to about four banks, and tried everything in my power to get a loan at any cost. I began to realize that I was not going to be able to get a loan nor get the AC fixed.

I began to panic because I knew it was summer and it was only going to get hotter. Every day I checked the forecast, to see how hot it would be, and unfortunately it did get hotter and hotter. I did not have any FAITH. I was putting my trust in the forecast rather than God. A lot of times we get sidetracked by our circumstances and we fail to realize that God is in control of each and every situation. Sometimes we forget who God is and that nothing is too hard for him (Jeremiah 32:27). Everything we go through in life is not a surprise to God. God knows what you are going to be battling against before it even happens to us.

After the first week I knew what to expect, and I stopped looking at the forecast because it was discouraging me. Out of nowhere I just got this birth of faith. After I got myself together and gave the situation to God my praying changed. I began to tell God that, "I know you are not going to leave my family hanging in the summer. My family are obedient children of God and tithe payers. How can God forget about people like that?" This also helped me with developing patience, which actually is one of the fruit of the spirits (Galatians 5:22-23). Something else I learned was that if you are waiting for something from God it is not so much how long you wait but how you wait. If you have a grumpy attitude and act like the situation is never going to get handled, then it won't.

I sat back one day and I realized I became so humble with the fact that we did not have any AC! It did not consume me like it had been in the beginning. It was like I kept complaining about it, checking the weather, and being sad at the thought of the loan not coming through. This experience taught me a lot on not to be PROUD OR ARROGANT. As quick as God has given you something, he can quickly take it away.

During this time I began to look for people in the bible that had humble characteristics. A very humble person in the Bible was Moses. Despite his feelings of inadequacy, Moses went through a lot and still put the Israelites before himself (Numbers 12:3). During this time Moses developed a strong and special relationship with God. God loves a humbled person. The Bible speaks of how humility comes before honor. God has promised to give grace to the humble while he opposes the proud (Proverbs 3:34). If we are content with situations and humble ourselves before God, that's when honor comes in.

When you are tested in dealing with honor, always go through the situation looking for the best. A lot of situations God puts you through usually help with humility, and a lot of times we are so distracted with the situation we forget about the meaning of them. Next time you are going through a test ask God what are you supposed to learn from it... And do not focus on the heat like me.

Chapter Two

In Those Jeans

So at my job I always listen to sermons and music via phone. It keeps me leveled and happy, so I won't have to worry about distractions. Well, for years I have been wearing these loose pair of pants. I really have not invested in a new pair of pants simply because I was not trying to impress anyone, and they would get dirty anyway. You see I work at a fast food restaurant so most of the time I would be getting dirty, and that's not the ideal job to look good at. Usually around 9:30 pm I would turn on a sermon, put my headphones in, and slide my phone into my back pocket. This has been my routine for years. After I listen to a sermon I would charge my phone up and then around 12 am I would pick my phone back up and listen to some Gospel music. Recently I had been talking about getting a new pair of work pants, and I finally decided to get a pair that I had seen a couple of my coworkers wear (they were actually yoga pants, and they fit so comfortably). While I was purchasing them I realized they did not have pockets, and the first thing that came to my mind was where will I put my phone when I'm at work. A lot of you may be asking what the BIG DEAL is. I work with my hands. I'm preparing food the entire time at work, so it is impossible for me to hold my phone during work. I could just sit my phone out on my station and play my music out loud, but it will only cause distractions for me, my coworkers, as well as the customers. My job is also very loud and if I want to hear and understand the information fully, I really need headphones.

I began to justify my actions and by saying, "I plan on only wearing these pants on morning shifts because I never listen to anything then because we are not allowed to have our phones out." But the funny part about that is I rarely work morning shifts. I was just fooling myself. This is when I began to realize I was in a test. A very small and easy one, but nevertheless, a test. I could easily say, "forget it," and just not wear the pants, but I spent money on them. And as you can guess I'm not going to let any of my money go to waste. So, me trying to be smart I still wore the pants to work, and it was the hardest thing I ever had to do trying to still listen to my sermons and music. I had to hold my phone in my hand. I even tried to make a case to put my phone into.

THIS WAS A TEST TO SEE WAS I GOING TO CONTINUE TO SEEK AFTER HIM. (Prov. 8:17).

And I realized that even if it is difficult I'm going to continue to seek after him. It's all about growth. You want growth so you can be prepared for situations that will test you; to see if you are diligently seeking after his heart; or those tight new pants you just brought.

Chapter Three

God Can Use A Sinner To Help You Grow Spiritually

Let me begin by saying that God can use anything to get your attention. Most people look for only preachers, ministers, and highly educated people to help them grow in life, but God does not work that way. God does not look for the qualified, he looks for the disqualified. While you are looking high above for someone, God is using people like babies (yes I said babies), homeless people, and drug addicts. If a person has the Word of God in their hearts why can't they share wisdom with other people?

One day I was randomly surfing through Instagram and I stumbled across the rapper "2 Chainz" page. I went to his page because I've heard he has a great personal chef, and since I'm interested in food, I took a look at some of his pictures. I eventually saw this post

> *"The Lord said, Do not be afraid. He is always with you. He has a band of Angels traveling with you everywhere you go. Before you enter into any environment ask God to set the atmosphere before you enter in. He hears your prayers and honors your prayers. You are the apple of His eye".*

I FELT LIKE THAT POST WAS MEANT FOR ME!!

The main part of the letter that stood out to me was "before you enter into an environment ask God to set the atmosphere." Ever since that day, anytime I go out I ask God to set the atmosphere. If I'm going to the mall I say, "God set the atmosphere in my car, on the roads, and at the mall." I started doing this on a daily basis to where now it is second nature.

A lot of people may say "You're not really doing anything", "that doesn't help", but it does. The Bible talks about speaking things into existence. Proverbs 18:21 (ESV) states that death and life are in the power of the tongue, and those who love it will eat its fruits.

You create your world with your words, and I want to create a positive life, so why not speak what I want. All the time I think about what the outcome of a lot situations would have been if I had not set the atmosphere. What if I was about to walk into robbery, but because I set the atmosphere there were angels there who protected me.

In this situation God used a "rapper" not only to show me, but to show the rest of the world the importance of speaking life. The person that wrote that note probably didn't even have a clue that it was going to affect a "fan" of the rapper 2 Chainz. Even though this rapper is using his gift in a way that may not be pleasing to God, one simple post changed my perspective on life! Just imagine how many other people were affected by that post as well.

A person should never look down on another person because they do not have the qualifications you think that they should have. Everyone wants to be used by God but no one is willing to step out. Make it your assignment to change someone's life, even if you think it is something small. Usually things that are small to us, are big to God. The Bible tells us not to despise small beginnings because the Lord rejoices to see the work begin.

Chapter Four

I Always Feel like Somebody's Watching Me

When you are a Christian and trying to live right, you had better believe people will be watching you. Some people will be watching you hoping for the best, and some praying on your downfall. I learned that it is best to represent God and not to make him look bad. When you were younger I'm pretty sure your parents used to always remind you to make a good impression on people and to not make them look bad because it reflects on them. And that is the same thing with God. A lot of us have given God a bad name. Have you ever wondered why people don't like going to church? Or why people don't like giving their tithes? Someone, somewhere did not represent God and led people to believe something false about him. A while ago my preacher made this statement, "Stop sinning online." He did not say that directly to me, he was speaking to the congregation. But, that made me think, "Have I sinned online." And sinning online can simply mean posting statuses or post that are ungodly.

So the other day I was on Instagram and I saw this post that was so funny and so true and I wanted to repost it. So I took a screen shot of the picture and for about an hour I debated if I should post it. I kept thinking about when my preacher said, "Stop sinning online." I thought about what my Christian followers would think, and what my worldly followers would think. I know a lot of people would call me a hypocrite. I even got to the point where I figured out a status to write under the picture. Something like "this so funny, I'm going to delete this post in a few because I know my Christian followers wouldn't like it." I was just trying to justify what I was about to do. But if I have to do all of that just to post a picture, it's not even worth it. Even though I don't have to explain myself to anyone but God I would rather not deal with it.

The post read, "My Vagina is tighter than yours."

THIS POST WAS WHAT THE FUSS WAS ALL ABOUT!! FUNNY RIGHT?

This was something that should be laughed at in private (and many of you may not understand the humor, but this post can potentially help someone who is battling with choosing to say the appropriate things on social networks). I knew it would have been hilarious to my peers. If I were to have posted this it would only confuse non-believers and have them think this is okay. First Corinthians 14:33 (NLT) states, "For God is not a God of disorder but of peace, as in all the meetings of God's holy people." Many older people may not understand the humor of this picture but it's actually referring to oneself as not "fast" as some other females may be (I know our generation is weird). This post in no shape or form promotes sex or promiscuity. I want to address something that I see a lot of my youth battling with online regarding what posts are okay to like, post, and comment on. We all know that our purpose is to represent God well, but just as my example stated, we can get so caught up in the fake social network world and trying to fit in, that for a split second, we can mess it all up.

The entire night I thought about why not posting the picture was a good idea. And the main reason was that people were watching and I didn't want anyone to be under the impression that "Johnelle did it, so can I." So the next day I get a text from a friend whom I totally forgot about. I met her through the app "Groupme." A friend of mine made a chat for young Christians around the area so we would be able to communicate with each other about God. We would all sometimes meet up at different places and do things together. It was a way to keep each other grounded. So, the text basically was about us catching up and talking about what we were doing with our individual ministries. As soon as we finished talking I realized that it was a sign from God. He was basically telling me that people are paying attention to me and that I was not even thinking about. If it had not been for that girl hitting me up, I would have totally forgotten she existed. God works in mysterious was to show you things and help you understand things better. Now, every time I look at that picture, I'm glad I didn't post it.

I'm quite sure that this chapter may rub a lot of adults the wrong way. But my only assignment here is to be transparent, share my story, encourage people, and pray that they understand things from my circumstances and mistakes. My purpose is not to make anyone uncomfortable or make you look at me as a HEATHEN simply because of a battle I choose to share.

Chapter Five

"Increase Was The Name That He Gave Me"

I'm always rapping that quote at work. It comes from a rapper name Jay-z, and I turned the words around. I changed my name to "Increase" a couple of months ago and it was the best decision ever (no, I didn't legally do it). Changing my name was basically another way for others, as well as myself, to speak life into me. A lot of worldly people may not understand the severity of speaking great things into a person and watching it come to pass. The idea of changing my name to Increase had nothing to do with me. It had everything to do with growing in God spiritually. One day I was at church and the prophetess at my church was speaking and she was talking about changing her name. She stated how she changed her name to Increase because she wanted an Increase from God. She even said she was going to change her name to "Wow", because when God is done with her people are going to say, "Wow". The increase doesn't have

33

to mean financially. A person can want an increase in faith, love, or even an increase in worshipping. After I left church that day I texted my best friend and said, "Let's change our names." Her response was, "No, why?" I began to break down what the sermon was about, and then she finally understood. I know that this may sound corny to some people but things like that excite me. As soon as I got home I changed my Facebook name, and then I wrote a post about what it meant.

Now, I know a lot of you may be thinking God could care less if a person changes their name or not, but actually God is known for doing a little name changing in the Bible himself. Two important people in the Bible whose names got changed were Abraham and Jacob. Most people are not aware that Abraham's name was originally Abram. Genesis 17:5 states, "What's more, I am changing your name. It will no longer be Abram. Instead, you will be called Abraham, for you will be the father of many nations." Everyone knows that Abraham had crazy faith, so what a better way for God to recognize his faith than by personally changing his name.

In another instance God also changed Jacob's name. After Jacob wrestled with an angel, he demanded a blessing from The Lord and the angel pronounced a blessing upon him, and a new name to go with it. Israel. This new name meant "he who prevails with God", or "May God prevail" (Genesis 35:10).

You see, changing someone's name is nothing new to God but, when people are not familiar with the bible it can throw someone for a loop. Changing your name can mean a new identity. When I became a new creature in Christ, I wanted to change my name. I did not want to be associated with my past, so the name Increase was great! Changing my name has not been easy though! I struggled with people laughing at me and even calling me crazy. I remember like it was yesterday when I first came to work and I told everyone my new name was Increase. They drilled me with questions and a lot of the answers were spiritual so I got to the point where I just stopped explaining it to them. Instead of everyone calling me Increase they decided to call me "decrease." It was funny in the beginning but then I realized that they were basically speaking negative things into my life. To this day sometimes my coworkers still call me decrease, and I really cannot do anything about it other than renounce it. Renouncing something means to refuse or reject something, and not let it take root in your life. Many people often throw around words simply because they do not understand the principle of how much power words carry. If people only understood how serious words were they would immediately stop using them incorrectly and in harmful ways.

I was at work one day and my coworker was calling my name, and I replied, "My name is Increase". So another coworker overheard this and he said, "That's not your name". So I began to say, "INCREASE WAS THE NAME THAT HE GAVE ME." I was not prepared for what he was about to say, then he looked at me and said, "Little girl, you need to stop playing with The Lord, you know he didn't give you that name". I just could not believe he said that, but it was typical coming from a worldly person with a worldly mindset. So I said, "Why do I have to be playing with The Lord? You don't believe I can hear from God? You don't think God wants an increase in my life? Is it because I'm young that you don't believe that God would tell me to change my name"? And obviously he didn't have anything to say. Well, actually he did but, he said he will get back with me and let me know (funny right). I've decided no matter what people say or do, if I want an increase in my life, I'm going to speak it. Often times we worry about someone's opinion that is clearly on their way to hell (and no I'm not talking about the guy in this example, just speaking in general). The only person we have to answer to is God and his opinion is all that matters. The more we focus on God the less of other people we should see.

Chapter Six

Fear

There are so many things that come to mind when I think of fear. To be honest there is a long list of things that put fear in my heart. I'm scared to sleep with my door open, scared to sleep in the dark, scared to stay home by myself. I was even scared to take a shower while I was home alone (well not anymore). Now, I have this list of things that I'm afraid of and I have no clue to why. Why am I afraid of all these things? Did something happen to me when I was young that I can't recall that causes me to have fear of so many things? To be honest, yes, something did happen to cause me to have this great amount of fear, and it was actually before I was born. I was in my mother's womb.

Have you ever seen a pregnant woman talk bad about a person, and they immediately stop talking and say, "Let me stop before something is wrong with my child". We have all heard these things. You don't have to be spiritual to understand this principle. Watch what you do and say, because you do not want your child to inherit "those" characteristics.

One day I sat back and thought about why I have so much fear. Then I realized that my mom has a lot of fear as well. Most of the things that I'm afraid of, she is afraid of as well. I did a little bit of research on my mom and found out that while she was pregnant with me she battled with fear in several of areas (unfortunately that part is not up for discussion). Fear is a spirit. And spirits are like leeches. Leeches travel, sucking blood out of a person. Let's think about fear being a leech for a moment. Fear would consume so much of a person to the point where there would not be any room for anything else. Imagine not being able to do anything because of fear keeping you trapped. That is kind of what happened to me.

Being that my mom was afraid of several things that spirit of fear transferred to me. I actually told my mom once that I got the spirit of fear from her, and boy did I not hear the end of that. See the thing about spirits and demons is that you can cast them out. Second Timothy 1:7 says, "For God has not given us a spirit of fear, but of power, and of love, and of a sound mind." You can choose life and choose not to live in fear. Many people think that just because you are battling with something you have to take crap from it, and you don't. The devil loves it when we let him take control of our lives. We need to put our foot down and let the devil know that he does not control us and neither does fear. Make a believer out of the devil and take back your freedom today.

I know I'm not a mother, but one thing that is for sure is that whatever you have in you will pour out of you, and in this instance it is fear pouring out onto a child. So, maybe the spirit you are dealing with is not fear, maybe its anger or depression. If you are carrying a child make sure you take an initiative to deal with these spirits so your child will not come under an attack as well. I learned this from T.D Jakes, demons travel in legions. Legions are a group of demons. The bible makes numerous references to a legion but one scripture that stands out to me is Mark 5:9 (ESV) which says, "And he (Jesus) asked him (the man), what is thy name? And he answered, saying, 'My name is Legion: for we are many.'" Since demons refer to themselves as being a Legion they will work together to destroy everything in sight. The devil wants control over territories. Not little small things but big things. Why do you think that in some states and cities they have strong spirits, such as California and New York, versus others where gambling and homosexual are promoted; like in Las Vegas (but that's a different story)? It's time we stop fighting our parents and grandparents demons. Break the generational curse. If you ever find yourself under attack with something that people in your family are dealing with as well, you need to pray against that spirit immediately, because if you don't, it will just travel through your family. Whatever comes out of you (give birth to) will deal with the same identical thing.

Chapter Seven

Patience

Patience is something we all should want. Not only because it helps us to better ourselves, it is actually a fruit of the spirit. Galatians 5:22 (NLT) states that, "But the Holy Spirit produces this kind of fruit in our lives; love, joy, peace, patience, kindness, goodness, faithfulness." Now, if the Bible speaks on it, it must be very important.

How do you know if you lack in patience? It's very simple. There are several ways to check. For example, if you are running late for work and you speed and curse every driver out, there's a good chance that you lack in patience. I lack in patience as well. I pray for patience so much that it is like second nature to me. One thing that I have learned is that when you pray for something, the devil is not going to be very far to test you about that particular thing.

I always pray for patience with my mom. Don't get me wrong, I love her but, sometimes I need the Lord to be with me when dealing with her. I started praying for patience with her about four months ago, and after that point, it seems like everything she does irritates me. I try to take it one day at a time. Every time I feel myself getting mad I just remind myself that this is just another test that I will not let the devil win. I know that it is the devil's goal to cause destruction in our family, so I try my best to recognize his tactics. A scripture that keeps me grounded through this trying time is Micah 7:6 (KJV) which states, "For the son dishonored the father, the daughter riseth up against her mother, the daughter-in-law against her mother in law; a man's enemies are the men of his own house". To be real with you, this scripture scares the living daylights out of me, and I refuse to be one of these people. Also, we all know the "famous" honor your mother and father scripture (honor them even when they are wrong and/or you may not fully understand their logic). Even if you don't go to church you should know that one.

Now I just tell myself, "Let it fly and keep it moving." But sometimes certain things can seem to get harder and harder. The more you carry yourself in a way as if it doesn't bother you, you will overcome. If a person does not pass the current test, the same one will be around the corner waiting for you. Now that I'm almost done with patience, I will not be surprised if I have another one to accomplish.

Chapter Eight

Not Listening To Others

There comes a time in your life when you have to stop listening to others and listen to God. God should be the only one that directs your steps. People will steer you in the wrong direction but God never will. Sometimes people may tell you things on purpose just to see you not prosper. The Bible strictly tells us the God has pleasure in our prosperity (Psalm 35:27). There have been plenty of times where people told me negative things about my future and it was my responsibility not to believe it. I began doing gospel rap maybe two years ago, and one guy at my job heard one of my songs and said, "You need to give it up". Now, I'm not about to say that I'm the best rapper out there but, I am rapping for God. It does not matter what other people may think about whether the way I'm praising God is good or not. I had the choice either to believe what the guy was saying or ignore the devil speaking through him. As you can see, a lot of the trials I go through happen at work. And to be quite honest, my coworkers probably never could understand what they put me through.

One thing I have learned while on this journey is to never ask God to rescue you from trouble. What good is it if every time something happens you are looking for God to bail you out? The best way to beat the devil at his own game is to ask God for strength. If no one else wants strength during their trials, give it to me, because I need strength for this trial and the next one. How can a person grow in the Lord during hard times if they are always getting rescued? That's just like a parent rescuing their child every time they come across a problem. That child would not understand how it feels to be a mature adult and understand how to deal with adversity.

Another big reason to listen to God and not other people is that GOD KNOWS WHAT HE IS DOING. He sees what everyone else can't. Ask yourself this, If God wanted you to do something would he really tell everyone? No. Something that has played in my mind numerous of times is the show "Preachers of LA." When that show first came out everyone and their momma was saying how they were playing with God, and how they were fake, and whatever else came to their mind. One thing I've learned while on this journey is to keep your mouth shut if you don't know something for sure. I refuse to slander someone and miss out on a blessing because of an assumption. While everyone was saying these guys are not real preachers no one knows what God told them to do. Let's say for example God told these guys to do this show to help people in their struggles, and to give people a different perspective of Christians. Why would God tell all of us (the world) his plan? It does not make since. Everyone, now a days, just wants to be in the loop of everything, and it just does not work that way.

There are many instances where God told me to do something and people (including adults) had a negative opinion. And there were times where I stopped listening to God (when I know I heard correctly) and listened to others simply because they were my elders. This set me back every time. Just because a person is an elder does not mean they have wisdom, can hear from God, and/or is living for God for that matter. Sometimes I can get so wrapped up into "I have to respect and listen to my elders" that I totally forget the instructions God has given me. If God wanted those people to know the plan he had for me, he would have told them. It's never anyone's business what God is up to. And believe me; God is always up to something.

Chapter Nine

Didn't I Tell You He's Not For You!

Have you ever tried your hardest to talk to someone and for whatever reason it did not work? That was God giving you a sign. There was this guy I was talking to and I really liked him. And before I began talking to him I asked God, "If you don't want me to talk to him give me a sign." This is where I messed up. Before I even got this guy's number I should have asked this, but I didn't. And I think this is what made it so hard for me to leave this guy alone. I never received a sign. So, in my mind I'm thinking, "Okay cool, I can talk to him. God didn't say no, but he didn't say YES either." One thing we should always pay attention to is to never ask God for a sign when dating because the signs are already there from the beginning. The Bible says you should know a person by their fruits. If their fruits are not of God (smoking, partying, drinking, etc.) then you should know better than to even ask God in the first place because you already have your answer.

As Christians we like to play dumb sometimes and I don't know why. We put ourselves in these tough situations and then we can't even get out of them. So, after talking to this guy for a little while, a little incident happened where he made a very rude remark about a guy I was working with. The guy I worked with heard of a prophesy and he told me, so I informed the guy I was talking to and his reaction was like he did not even know God. It made me very angry to the point where I told him I didn't want to talk to him anymore. If I would not have talked to him in the first place I would not have had to deal with that situation.

Months passed and I still wanted to talk to this guy after the fallout. I used some drastic measures to get his attention. Might I add, I knew this guy was interested in me so I was not worried. But it seemed like every time I tried to get his attention, or get someone to ask about "us," it never worked out according to my plan. Things always went to the left. I tried getting this guy to talk back to me at least six times, and every time it did not work. It got to the point where I started saying, "It's not meant for me to talk to him, and God knows exactly what he's doing." And quite frankly I knew what he was doing as well but, I did not want to accept it. I got desperate to the point where I started to give God a preposition (I know y'all are probably thinking I'm crazy now). You know you are bad off when you try to "trick" God. I do not know who I was trying to fool, but it was not working. But nothing ever worked out until one day....

Me and some friends were going out so I invited this guy and he came (I told you he was interested). Afterwards we all went to my friend's dorm room and started arguing about how things did not work out between us, then the conversation shifted and we started to talk about God. When we started talking about God I felt good, and I felt as if I had won him over. I even got to the point where I told myself that "God wanted this to happen." So, after this happened I was sure that we were meant to be in each other's lives. But two days later, everything went salty and I was confused. I eventually had enough and I got tired of making a fool of myself. Months passed and I was talking to one of my friends about the situation and he told me, "Rejection is God's way of protection". Ever since that day I have yet to bring this guy's name up (well sometimes). I ignored God for so long because I wanted to talk to a guy so bad. I wasn't even thinking the whole situation through. This guy could have been the death of me. I was only looking at the outside and not looking at his heart with God. This guy could have easily pulled me in and turned my life around for the worse. Females always have the intentions of changing a guy, but it always turn into the guy changing the female.

There will be plenty of times when the devil will try to come in and cloud your vision. But, the main goal should always be to remain focused and keep the "randoms" out of your life. A random is a person you call when you're bored; don't have anyone to talk to, or just a person used to fill a void. I learned the term "random" from a famous preacher name Heather Lindsey. She is "dope," and she always preaches and blogs to young women about relationships and how to build a stronger relationship with God. God cannot work fully with you if you always have someone in the area where he belongs. From then on I started praying about everything. I do not even care about having "bait" (potential guy friends) anymore. My relationship with God is more important.

Recently, I was tested in that area. I gave a guy my number and we began texting and I told God, "Give me a sign if you don't want me to talk to him." The next day he texted me something inappropriate and I was happy I got my answer. So, it was my decision to be obedient.

Being obedient goes a long way. If you stay true to God he will make sure your blessings come at the right time. Exodus 19:5 (NLT) states, "Now if you obey me fully and keep my covenant, then out of all nations you will be my treasured possession. Although the whole earth is mine".

Now, you would think that after this incident I would have learned my lesson but, that's not the case. Some of us can be extremely hard headed. A guy from my past came back up in my life, and wanted to hang out and catch up. I have learned that if a guy is in the past, he is in the past for a reason, and he belongs there as well. Anyway, I forgot everything I had learned and started chillin' with him. I brought up God and talked about my purpose in life and I also tried to get him to think about his eternal life. No matter who I deal with I always make it known that I'm a Christian who loves God and I am not one of these phony ones. Everything was going cool with this guy but, I knew deep down inside that he would only bring me down and I could not be around him too long. I tried to pressure God onto him, but it would not work. I told him he should come to church with me, that his whole life would change forever but who was I fooling. The friendship was starting to get the best of me due to a lot of characteristics he had. For starters he smoked, drank, partied weekly, confused about God, and lacked commitment in almost every area. I know you may be thinking, "How she can be attracted to something like that?" But, to be honest it really is not hard when your flesh is in control. I eventually cut all ties with this guy because the friendship was not bringing forth any fruit. To be honest, I was a little sad. I liked him but I knew how the outcome would be. If I had been obedient in the beginning I would have saved myself a lot of trouble and headache. We put ourselves in situations then ignore God and then pray to him about the problems we have. Should he even answer us after all that? Even though we treat God like he is nothing, he still looks at us as the apple of his eyes.

Chapter Ten

Recognize The Little Things

Sometimes In life we can get so consumed with everything that is going on that we tend to forget to count our blessings. Every day that we wake up on earth is a blessing, and God deserves a "Thank you." Have you ever heard of the saying everything happens for a reason? This saying sometimes can be clichéd because it is used so much, but it is actually true. I was listening to a Joel Osteen sermon a while ago and he was basically breaking down how God puts things in place for a reason. Think about a time you overslept for work and you had to rush and get ready but still arrived late. Situations like this make a person very irritated and angry. But, think about why God was trying to get you to recognize something small as being late for work. God could have been trying to protect you from an accident, drunk driver, or even from getting a ticket while on the road.

Every time things like this take place I try to look at the bigger picture and see if there was a blessing in this.

Recently I had a very important doctor's appointment which was scheduled on a Wednesday evening. My doctor contacted me to reschedule my appointment because of a last minute meeting a week in advance. Meanwhile my manager scheduled me to work that Wednesday morning (the day I was supposed to have had my appointment). Mind you I never work morning shifts, but for some odd reason I had to work. After I got off of work I drove around the corner and my steering wheel got very stiff and I could not turn the wheel. Since the speed limit was maybe around 15 miles per hours I was okay, and able to pull over safely. The whole time in my mind I was mad at the world. I did not even take time to realize the blessing. Because of what happened I could not see it. I then got my car towed to a local shop to get it repaired.

At the end of the day I set back and realized, "Dawg, how could I have missed this blessing." It seemed so small to me that I did not even recognize it. Let's rewind and take it back for a second. What if I had not had to work that morning; and what if my doctor's appointment never got cancelled? I would have been driving 45 minutes to another city to the doctor's office while driving 65 mph. My steering wheel would have locked up on me and I could have been in a potentially serious accident. God knew exactly what he was doing. I was mad because my plans were messed up, but God was cleaning up my mess before it even had happened. Fast forward back in the story. I dropped my car off to the repair shop on a

Wednesday and got it back on a Friday. That Sunday my mechanic got killed in a car accident. The point of me informing you guys about this part is because this was a blessing as well (not the death part). Let me put you up to speed. My car took two days to get fixed because the shop had a hard time finding the piece my car needed and it had to get shipped from out of state. If that shipment had arrived one day later, my car would not have gotten fixed and I would have not been getting my money reimbursed to me. See, God knows the end of every situation and if you are surely his child he will keep you in perfect peace. Luke 4:10 (NLT) states, "He will order his angels to protect and guard you."

We have so many blessings to be thankful for. Every day you wake up and every night you go to sleep remind yourself of the blessings in your life. And if that's not enough and you think that's not worthy, think about yourself as a blessing. Your loved ones cherish and love you, and having family is a blessing itself. There are numerous people who would do anything to know how it feels to have a loving and caring family. Just because your family does not seem special to you, someone somewhere is praying for that special thing.

Chapter Eleven

Monkey See, Monkey Do

Growing up it's our parent's job to instill positive things in our lives that will help us down the road in our life such as; getting an education, respecting others, and keep God first. We all have certain habits we partake in and most of the time we never know why we really do them. Years down the line I want to be able to say, "Man, I'm glad that I was taught these things," and hopefully be a blessing to others. One thing for sure is that children pay attention to everything. The things that parents may not think we understand we actually do. I remember when I was about nine years old, and my dad was preaching one day at church and he described how everyday he wakes up he says, "Lord, I thank you." Now, I really did not know what that meant at that age, but I made sure ever since that day I said the same thing. Now that I'm older and I think about what I'm saying, I'm surprised simply because you're not going to catch too many nine year olds catching on to spiritual things as such. I really consider that a blessing.

Ever since I could remember my mom walks around the whole entire house anointing our heads, praying over the whole house, opening and closing the doors in the house, to get the demons out, and turning every TV on in the house to the gospel channel. I used to hate it. I used to wake up with an attitude because I could not stand to have the TV on so loud. What I did not understand was that my mom was imparting something in me, and I did not notice it until years later. One day my parents were out of town and I woke up early and realized that the TV wasn't on, and I had not been prayed for. So, I turned on every TV in the house to the gospel channel and turned the volume up extra loud. Then I walked around the whole house praying and opening and closing doors commanding the devil to leave. After I finished doing all of that I just started laughing. I could not believe that everything my mom did rubbed off on me like that. But, to be honest, I don't regret it, because one day I will have my own house and family and who will do it then? That's why it is always good not to forget where you came from. Proverbs 22:6 (NLT) tells us to "direct your children onto the right path, and when they are older, they will not leave it".

Just sit back and think about all the old remedies that our grandparents taught us that we still keep up with today. Have you ever just sat back and wondered, "What's the real reason of cooking black eyed peas for the New Year?" But, I bet you still cook them though? When I grow old I want to be able to sit back and realize that everything I learned was not in vain. I want people to remember me for the positive things I contributed to their lives. One thing that I will never forget is my preacher saying (and I may not quote it the exact same way) "You should be thankful for the person that invited you to church." Think about the time you got saved. Who invited you? What if you never would have come to church that day? All these things play a role somewhere, somehow. I want people to remember me as the person that cared about people's eternal lives, and maybe someone will try to duplicate what I tried to do and save some souls.

Chapter Twelve

I Mean.... People Are Gonna Talk

While on this journey I realized that everyone talks and people you would not even believe will run your name down in the dirt. You think that when you become saved everything will be all good, but actually people will treat you like you sold your soul or something. For the most part you will get love from your brothers and sisters in Christ but, that small percentage doesn't compare to what you will be dealing with in the world. When I began this journey I never knew it would be this hard. I've been called a hypocrite so many times, I began to believe it. What people don't understand is that this walk is a process. Nothing happens overnight. Do you really think you are going to give your life to God and Satan isn't going to turn the heat up on you? One thing I learned to do is put a deaf ear to people. Most of the people that open up their mouth are not aware or fully realize that they are being used by the devil. Discernment is the key.

Having discernment can help you to understand if the devil is working through a person and if you should keep your mouth closed or not.

Satan's plan is to get you off course, so if he can get people to plant negative seeds into your life you will potentially believe it. Also, everything that people say is not meant for you to comment on. See, you have five minute arguments which are pointless. These are small arguments that you fuss for about five minutes then it's done. Never entertain these things. They can be about something as small as the remote control, lights being left on in the house, or music playing too loud.

Then there are hour long arguments. They are not worth it either, simply because a person can literally drag an argument on for so long after it should have been over with. These arguments can be about gas money or even bills. Anything longer than those are considerably more important to a point. Arguments should NOT last longer than an hour, and if you find yourself going back and forth with someone in this situation you should just end it there.

A reaction is all that people want from you most of the time when they talk. Their goal usually is to see how quick they can get you to sin so they can call you a hypocrite. One thing that I'm working on is to keep my mouth closed regardless of the situation. Even if they are making me look weak, silence is the best solution. The Bible talks about how you should not go back and forth with a fool because you will then look like one as well.

There comes a point in life when Christians have to get off the milk and start eating meat. Eat the meat and spit out the bones. That simply means that certain things should not get under your skin. If you are growing in Christ, at some point you have to put a deaf ear to some things.

There have been several instances where I have known that people were talking about me. One thing that I think that hurt the most was that some of the people who were talking, I wasn't prepared to believe they did it. As time passed I realized that I couldn't control what everyone said, but I could control how I represented God. Plenty of times I had to bite my tongue and not say what I really wanted to say. I knew better, so I did not stoop to someone's level just to degrade them, and risk a possible blessing. One thing I learned from Joel Osteen is that we are pearls. Everything we go through is to help us and mold us to become the perfect shape. When people talk about me now I usually smile or say something slick like, "Do you really mean that?" or "I'm gonna make you eat those words." You see people don't understand the power of not touching God's children. First Chronicles 16:22 (KJV) states, "touch not my anointed, and do my prophets no harm." I don't think people understand that if you mess with God's child, you will have to face consequences. God will not let someone get away with negative behavior towards his children.

Sometimes we feel like we have to put someone in their place and straighten them out but, actually, we should let God fight our battles. If we just do what we are supposed to do, then he can do what he's supposed to do. Now, what I try to do when someone talks about me is just remember that they don't know any better. I will not get anywhere by trying to go back and forth with the enemy (the enemy is the one using them). Peace is what we all should be pursuing. If we have peace in our heart we can bet that small situations as such will not bother us so much.

People can stoop so low sometimes just to get under your skin. As you begin this walk people will just PICK. Anything they can find, they will pick at you to get you to break. I dealt with this on several occasions, even till this very day. All it takes is for me to say one thing and someone will just twist my words around. People can be so quick to tell you what the Bible says and how your actions do not line up with God, but they are not even living even a little bit for Christ. WATCH OUT FOR PEOPLE LIKE THAT!

Chapter Thirteen

What Does God Want?

One thing we need to always keep in mind is what God wants. We can get so wrapped up in our own lives that we forget about what God has for us. Sometimes we need to sit back and just say, "Lord, let your will be done." Now, after you say this don't expect for your life to be the same. The devil will come at you from every angle, but it's only because you asked God to step in and help guide you. We all struggle with why things are not going as planned in our life but know we have not fully obeyed God.

For about two years I thought God wanted me to write an autobiography. I got to the fourth page and I couldn't find anything else to write. I struggled and I began to think I was not focused or maybe I did not have enough enthusiasm for the project. I was wrong. I began to pray that God anoint my book (sounds weird being that I didn't even have one). With faith you have to speak things into existence, even if it looks crazy. A couple of months ago I wanted to try something new, so I began to write little sermons. At the time I was doing it because I just thought God was getting me prepared for my future, so I didn't pay it much attention. I would label each entry as sermon 1, 2, 3 and so forth. By the time I got to the fourth sermon I realized that it was not meant to be sermons, but a blog. I got so excited because I always wanted to do a blog. As I began to start the process of blogging everything went wrong. The blog websites never worked for me, and my computer started to shut off. My first thought was the devil is a liar! When most people face adversity their first instinct is to quit. I refused to quit, I have never been a quitter. So, I continued to write, not knowing what the ultimate purpose was, or who I was writing too. One day God told me that I would be writing a book. I got super excited because a book was the last thing that I was thinking about.

When you are obedient and do the things God tells you to do, you will always reap the benefits. I could have easily said, "Well, I don't know what I'm writing for so I'll just stop right here." And that's what the devil usually wants. He wants us to quit before our breakthrough. God knows exactly what he's doing. Most of the time he just wants us to see that he has a good plan. The Bible says in Philippians 1:6 (NLT), "And I am certain that God, who began the good work within you, will continue his work until it is finally finished on the day when Christ Jesus returns."

Two years ago I was so concerned with writing a book, and I didn't even ask God if that was his will. In life we all get off course trying to do what we want to do, then get mad if things don't go accordingly. Staying in God's will can prevent so many things, believe it or not. Imagine if I had written that book, it would have been horrible. To begin with I was not as knowledgeable as I am now, I lacked the resources at the time, and to be honest I wasn't living 100% for God like I should have been. How can I write about God and not live for him in my actions.

If I can encourage anyone today, I recommend reading Matthew 6:33 (KJV) which states, "Seek ye first the kingdom of God, and his righteousness; and all these things should be added unto you." If you follow God's guidelines everything you need and want will fall into place.

Chapter Fourteen

Friendships

Growing up as a child you are always told that good friends are hard to come by, so when you get a good friend hold on to them. When I began this journey I had several friends and I never thought that these people would not walk this road with me. What babies in Christ fail to realize is that while you are transforming into what God wants you to become you will lose friends. Sometimes you can't take old friends into new seasons. Sometimes it may seem as a loss because we became so used to a person, but God is all-knowing and he knows what's best for us. You may be asking yourself, "Why is it so crucial that I end old friendships?" One thing I've learned is that bad friendships are like poison. When you are trying to do the right thing it's always best to have a friend to encourage you to do better.

One thing that I battled with is dealing with the loss of my friends. Many people think that if they are no longer a friend with a person they have to be a bad person and that's not the case. When I was beginning this journey I lost many friends. I'm a decent person and I surrounded myself with no less than standup people, so you can understand why I was a little devastated. I saw plenty of my peers changing their lives around and their close friends were doing the same thing. I questioned God several times as to why that couldn't be my friends and I? Why couldn't my friends become saved as well? But, God knows what's in front of us and he knows what's best for us. Cutting my friends off was very hard for me and it can be hard for anyone who has a close relationship with a person. In the beginning, I didn't think that them being in my life was a problem but I soon realized that I could not talk to them about God like I wanted to. I started to feel uncomfortable bringing up testimonies and situations where I knew God was intervening. Something that a good friend of mine shared with me was that "if someone makes you feel uncomfortable when talking about God, you don't need them in your life."

My friendships got to the point where we were holding onto it by a thread. I knew the time was approaching where I had to put an end to the friendship but I didn't know how. One day I was at church and I received prayer and my pastor told me that God was going to cut some people out of my life that's not adding to it, and most definitely he did. None of my friendships ended in a dramatic or negative way. It was more of an unspoken thing. We all ended on good terms. But, one friend in particular hurt me the most to let go simply because I knew she didn't have a strong relationship with God nor Godly influences in her life. Months after the friendship ended I began having dreams about her. And these were not just regular dreams.

In every dream she was trying to befriend me, and it got to the point where the dreams were occurring on a weekly basis and I began to get scared. I really did not understand why I kept having dreams about her because in every dream she was persistent to be back as my friend. The only thing I could do for the first couple of months was pray because I didn't understand what was going on. So, once again I went to receive prayer and my preacher told me that "you can't trust everyone and everyone is not your friend. God is going to reveal to you who to watch out for." The dreams continued to happen, even to this day I have dreams but, now I'm more content with them and I understand God is just trying to protect me. Now, he's not saying she's an evil or bad person, but it's quite obvious that I need to keep my distance. Recently my friend had a housewarming party and she was there. I didn't feel uncomfortable or anything. I paid my respects and kept it moving. I know some our mutual friends thought maybe it was an opportunity to make amends and become friends again, but that was not on my agenda. I also knew that the devil was present and he wanted things to go his way, but that was not going to happen either. If God wants something to work out he will make a way.

One thing that I learned is that never take losing friends as a loss. God will always restore you and make sure he gives you double for your trouble. For about a year prior to this incident I began to pray for new friends. Now, praying for friends this long can be irritating and exhausting but, I knew that I needed new friends ASAP. I was literally about to go crazy. Fortunately, God has good timing and I met a whole new set of friends by the summer time. I had this friend who made up a Christian chat room, where we all could converse with each other. There were plenty of times where many of the other people expressed how they prayed to God for new friends and then the Christian chat room came together. Even after that point I made more friends that were beneficial to my walk with Christ.

When growing apart from someone you don't have to have bad blood with the person. Even though I'm not friends with my old friends anymore I still pray for them. Even though they are not in my presence anymore I will always wish them the best of luck, and pray that they find peace in God. If that old friend chooses to drag your name in the dirt or just talk negative against you, then that will forever be their problem. I refuse to let someone hinder my blessings over something as small as a friendship that can be replaced. The bible talks about focusing on heavenly things instead of earthly things. I recommend you set your mind to pleasing God and being obedient and when you do these things everything else will line up. Also prayer should be the number one priority used to focus on God's will.

God will always open doors for new avenues for friends. At times I can be very judgmental of who I surround myself with. I want those I surround myself with to have some of the same characteristics and features that I like and enjoy. For example; having the same style in clothes, music, and personality is important to me. Sometimes we pray to God for things such as FRIENDS and he gives them to us but not the way we want them. God knows what's best for us so sometimes that friend that's into clothes and music can push you towards making those things into your idol. I had to learn the hard way. I was constantly pushing new friends away. I knew that I was praying to God for Christian friends but, when I got them I really did not want them because they did not look nor act like me. However, you guys know we serve a humbling God, so, it got to the point where I could not make them into who I wanted them to be. I had to be content with my new friends. Don't get me wrong I love my friends, but if I had to choose them on my own it's a good chance I would be lonely. These new friends of mine bring great things to the table, and they opened my mind to new things.

One new friend of mine in particular is the total opposite of me. We bump heads constantly but, I'm blessed to have him as a good friend because he's very educated, well rounded, and challenges me spiritually. Actually they all push me to become a better person and above all else they love God. Something that I learned during this process is that sometimes God has to get you alone to deal with you. There's a difference between being lonely and being alone. Lonely is a state of mind caused from being isolated. Being alone is simply being separated from other people. We can be so distracted with other people, and refuse to realize that we are not spending any time with God. And that's all God wants from us is to spend time with him. Either we can do it on our own or God will just have to do it for us. Being alone is not a bad thing when your time is devoted to God. When God gets us in this position the enemy will try everything to get you to believe negative thoughts. But the Bible tells us in Deuteronomy 31:8 that God will never leave us nor forsake us, do not fear or be dismayed. Fortunately God has good timing and I met a whole new set of friends that changed my life.

Chapter Fifteen

Being Called Crazy

One thing that I deal with on a regular basis is being called "crazy." Now, of course I'm not crazy, but sometimes I can get a little crazy when I speak on the topic of God. I learned that if you are passionate enough about something, if someone disrespects it on any level, it's going to cause some type of a reaction. I always hear people discussing things in the Bible or just talking about things in the body of Christ that really make me mad. Most of the time people do not have the proper knowledge in this area but they continue to talk like they have everything figured out. I have been working on keeping my mouth shut, but when topics like this come up I have to say something. Now, there are different levels of crazy that people may confuse you with being but, let me be the first to tell you about how crazy I am about Jesus.

I'm crazy about Jesus. I'm basically a Jesus freak. Most of the time when I open up my mouth I'm usually bringing his name up, or how he has blessed me. When the world hears a person constantly talking about Jesus it becomes a problem. Even though everyone claims to really love Jesus they do not really want to hear you express it. The world makes the love of Jesus seem like a bad thing whereas people hold a higher standard for treasures on this earth.

Then we have the defensive crazy. With the defensive crazy you are defending something or someone you truly care about. If someone does something regarding this person you may get a little crazy. For example, you have a close family member who you truly love, you find out someone has been picking at them so you "GET CRAZY." Now, you are not really crazy mentally but, the fact that someone thinks it's okay to disrespect a loved one makes you have to express your emotions in a way that may seem crazy. I fall under the category of defensive crazy. I'm always finding myself defending God, the Bible, and Christians. I hate the fact that people find it hard to understand or even want to understand God. If I see a negative post on a social network I speak on it. If I hear someone at work disrespecting God, I speak on it as well. I feel as if it's my duty to address things that are not clear. Most of the time I may handle the situations inappropriately but my intentions are always good. I try my best to explain things in love and being that I'm so passionate about God my reactions can be intense. I do not go as far as to ridicule a person but "the kid be feeling it." Have you ever noticed how a coach acts during an important game? They are into it like they are actually the ones playing. That's the same way I act about God when explaining things to people, as if I'm the one that is headed to HELL.

To this day, one thing that I'm working on is preaching to people in love. A lot of people will not be willing to listen to you preach because they feel as if they can't learn anything from you. But as long as you are on this earth there is something that can be learned. All I ever hear at work is, "Why should I listen to you?", and, "You are no better than me." We all have something to learn and grow from no matter what stage in our walk we are in. Our job as Christians, while we are on this earth, is to help other people with our knowledge. Do not miss out on a blessing just because you are scared to be a blessing.

Chapter Sixteen

Believe In Yourself When No One Else Does

My preacher once preached a sermon and he said we should never stop dreaming. I think a lot of people get to a certain age and they feel as though dreaming is for children, but there is not a cut off age. Have you ever sat back and thought about how while you were growing up adults used to always ask, "What do you want to be when you grow up?" And no matter how weird the answer was they would always reply and say something like, "The sky's the limit." Who made it appropriate to shoot a person's dream down? As I get older I realize that I have to guard my heart and I can't tell just anyone my dreams. People do not care about your dreams the way that you do.

About two years ago I decided that I wanted to become a gospel rapper. This was a new found dream, not in a million years would I guess that I would rap for the Lord. In the beginning I was telling everyone that I wanted to be a gospel rapper and that God had given me several signs that it would come to pass. I was excited, and everyone around me could tell. I used to say things to my coworkers like, "I'm not going to be working here much longer." Or, when people asked me when I would graduate from college I would say, "I'm not graduating." It got to a point where people began to laugh at me or either give me their personal opinion on life. What God has for you it is for you. So, no matter what anyone has to say, it should not matter, as long as you know what God told you. From the time I began rapping until now, I still have to deal with people trying to shoot down my dreams. The devil always finds a way to throw darts at you to discourage you, but it's our responsibility to recognize his tactics. There have been several instances where I had to encourage myself and believe the promise God had given me, even when my loved ones didn't. It can be very hard not getting the support you feel you deserve but, situations like that always helps in developing you into a stronger fighter for Christ.

There were plenty of times I have had to redirect my thinking towards positive things. Sometimes I find myself getting irritated because I expect people to believe in me the same way I do. There have been several occasions where people have caught me off guard with their opinions and suggestions for my life, and many older people may say I'm being stubborn or hard headed but I choose to say I have childlike faith. I will not have it any other way.

Recently, my dad came and told me I should work on getting some credit. To be honest I did not want to hear it because why would I need credit for if I'm going to be a MILLIONAIRE. Now, many of you may think that that's too extreme but, the Bible speaks of God having pleasure in our prosperity and I'm just speaking it into existence. When I hear people close to me speak about my future as if I need a backup plan it is hard to deal with. People love it when they have a strong support system and they stick with them through thick and thin. My thing is that I don't want to just pick certain things in the Bible that I want to believe and other things aren't that important. If the bible says I can have prosperity, and it says, "Ask and it shall be given" (Matthew 7:7 ESV), then that is what I'm going to do. That's what we all should do! We let what other people say bring us down, and in all honesty we should go hard for the things we want even if no one wants to believe. One thing that I always tell people is that, "You're not going to be saying that when I'm rich." When you make a believer out of someone they will always remember the negative things they said to you.

Another instance was when my mom and sister was discussing on how to get me this job as a merchant seaman (a good paying government job). They were telling me how much I could make and the connections that they had. I wasn't trying to hear it. I began saying that I'm going to be a famous gospel rapper and I already know what I'm going to be. They began to tell me that I needed a backup plan and asking me what I was going to do if it didn't work out. I always get a little down when I hear Christians speak in a negative way. We go to church every week and learn all these lessons on what we should work on and how to stomp all over the devil's head, but we never use what we learn. I guess we are supposed to use them when it's only convenient for us. It's always good to have the word of God instilled in us for times when we are in a battle. You may be asking yourself, "How is this a battle?" Anytime someone or something tries to come in between what is bringing you closer to God, my friend, it's definitely a battle. The main goal is to continue to push and ignore the things that are not pleasing to God. And to be quite honest, it does not take a rocket scientist to figure out that the enemy does not want you to do what is pleasing to God.

God loves it when we believe in ourselves. We shouldn't wait around for someone to push us or tell us what a good idea is or not. You can't have the whole world believing in you when you don't even believe in yourself. Believing is an inside job. Just think about all the famous celebrities that made it this far. What if they waited around for someone to believe in them, they actually would never be famous! The devil loves it when you are complacent and stagnant waiting for something that's never going to happen. Give the devil a black eye and show him whose boss by believing today.

Chapter Seventeen

Don't Be Scared To Stand Up For Christ

One thing that I've noticed about this generation is that they are scared to stand up for what is right. They will defend everything in their power except for Christ. After all Jesus has done for us we shouldn't mind sacrificing some things for a greater purpose. We need to be aware that in our daily lives we are not to be ashamed of God. "For whoever is ashamed of me and my words in this adulterous and sinful generation, of him will the son of man also be ashamed when he comes in the glory of his father with the holy angels" (Mark 8:38, ESV). I don't know about anyone else but, I don't want to have to experience Jesus being ashamed of me. I want to make him happy and proud. I want to do things for God where I know I put a smile on his face. If there is a cause or a situation where I have to stand up for Christ I will do so.

Recently I had to stand up for Christ and I was so proud of myself. I was at work talking about God, as usual, to a couple of my coworkers and I received a complaint from a customer. Now, the complaint wasn't fully about me talking about God but more so of a side note. The complaint was about an order that I "supposedly" made incorrectly. I work at a fast food restaurant and people come in and out of the store complaining of how the food is not made properly or how the order isn't made correctly. On this specific day a customer said that we did not make her sandwich the way she asked, so my coworker came to me and told me about the order and we had a small conversation about how I did make it properly or maybe he just rung the order up incorrectly. Now this may seem irrelevant to the story but customers come in the store all the time and lie about orders so it can be a bit frustrating. What I did not know at the time was that the lady overheard the whole conversation. The lady called the 1-800 number and complained about us discussing her order, but she also added that we were talking about Jesus. I honestly felt like the last part was uncalled for and it did not have anything to do with the situation. I guess, in her mind if I had not been talking about Jesus I would have gotten her order correct.

Two days later I get to work and my manager asked to speak with me in her office. I had a write up waiting for me. The district manager called the store to make sure I received a write up. I couldn't believe that they were taking it that serious. What I really couldn't believe was that the customer added the part about Jesus into the complaint as if talking about Jesus was wrong. To be honest I didn't even let the situation get me mad, I just signed my write up with a smile on my face. For some reason I was happy. I got persecuted because of Jesus and I felt good. Matthew 10:22 (ESV) states that, "and you will be hated by all for my names sake. But the one who endures to the end will be saved." This scripture gave me so much hope that I didn't worry about what it looked like in the physical. The situation was so overwhelming that I began telling my coworkers about what had happened. Everyone's reaction was the same. They could not believe that I had gotten written up for talking about Jesus. It got to a point where everyone started voicing their opinion on what "they would have done." I didn't entertain the conversation the rest of the employees were having because it was pointless and I did not want to mess up my blessing by running my mouth. I then posted a status on Facebook and Instagram just to share what just occurred. Everyone that commented on my post responded from a carnal mind. People are so quick to voice their opinion on what they would do when they are mad and forget about what Jesus wants you to do. While on this walk it specifically states in the Bible that a part of following Christ is that you WILL be persecuted, so what's the purpose of going against it. Just accept it. While people were telling me their views on this situation I was just looking back and saying to myself, "That's why you're still in the same position you were in last year." God deals with every one of his children in many different ways. And the way he deals with us is not anyone's business. At some point in our walk we will be tested and the only way you can pass the test is to achieve a level of knowledge in a particular area so you can move on to the next level. I put a lot of thought into what would have happened if I had handled the situation differently. I would literally be right back in the same position dealing with the same thing again. It's always best to learn from a situation the first time.

There used to be a point in my life where I felt as if I needed to voice my opinions and suggestions. But what is that really proving. I have to remind myself that people are looking up to me and I have to be an example. Believe it or not people do not read the Bible anymore. Sometimes you will be the only Bible people will read, showing Christians, as well as unbelievers, the proper way to handle problems as Christ would. Don't get me wrong it may not be easy but as you grow in The Lord, God will give you kingship over your flesh. Always do the opposite of what your flesh wants. Starve your flesh so God can live in you so you can stand up for Christ.

Chapter Eighteen

When It Seems Like Living For God Isn't Enough

Many times people think living for Christ is going to be easy and it will be a piece of cake, but that's far from the truth. In the beginning, it definitely can be trying because that's when you are attempting to find your identity. All you ever want is for someone to understand you and the mission at hand. I remember when I wanted to do something for God, way before the rapping came about. My best friend and I started having Bible study every week at my house for some of our peers. In the beginning, a good amount of people showed up, but eventually people stopped coming. Even friends stopped showing up. Now, I always thought that friends were supposed to have your back through thick and thin, but that didn't happen. I could not understand why I felt the way I did when I was doing something for God. Sometimes you get to the point where you feel like you are better off not saved because it's like pulling teeth due to the respect you have for Christ. I learned that just because you have love and respect for God it doesn't mean everyone else will. Just because you are doing everything right for God, worldly people could care less.

The Bible tells us to guard our heart and that's the best advice to take, religious or not. Those things that you care for and love, such as God and your spiritual relationship with Christ, should be guarded from worldly people, and even some Christians. Christians will let you down just as quickly as worldly people. Being that I love God, and love going to church, and love making gospel music, also means that someone somewhere does not care about any of that.

As I was saying in the previous chapters I listen to sermons and gospel music while I'm at work. One day I was at work with my headphones in and my manager started to complain about me not doing teamwork, and how I couldn't complete orders because I had my headphones in. In her words, "Maybe I could get the orders correct if I didn't have my headphones in." To be honest that cut me deep because I was listening to something that had to deal with God. People that I surround myself with on the daily basis that proclaim to believe in God show me otherwise. I guess that God is important but not so much in this situation. I always expect people to be in agreement with me since I'm doing something positive. This can be so discouraging at times. We feel as though people should respect and honor God just as you do, but that's not the case.

Pushing ourselves for Christ should always be a priority. There will be times when no one else is around and we have to go hard for God alone. If you are out there living for God for attention, you are in the wrong game. We need to already expect people to let us down so we can simply understand that God will never do that to us. No matter how nice, or humble, or saved you are, living for God sometimes is not enough for some people. You can't please everyone. And, just because you don't get a point in your "managers" book for being obedient to Christ and listening to his word, you will get a point from God. Having your name put in the lamb's book of life should be your ultimate goal, and no one should stop just because of what someone else thinks.

There will come a point where living for God can get so frustrating that you end up falling. No one ever has the intention on falling on purpose, but the pressure sometimes can be so great that the result is sin. I have felt like living for God wasn't filling the void that the Bible speaks about. It felt like I was missing out on my youth. If you are a baby in Christ people know that you are not knowledgeable in many areas, and it will show in your actions. In the very beginning, when I started this walk I was getting tugged from left to right. My birthday was coming up so I wanted to do something fun and new. I decided to have a stripper party. Now I knew people were going to look at me funny because the day before that I was just talking about God. Deep down I knew that I should not have had that party but, all I could think about was that having a stripper party was on my bucket list and I wanted to have one before I started living completely for God. And that's how carnal our minds can be sometimes. I never even considered the misfortunes and consequences that night could have carried. After that night I felt low, and people began to say I was playing with The Lord. What I'm trying to get at is that nothing will ever be enough for this world, that's why it's our responsibility to seek more of Christ daily. Our confirmation should only come from God. And if insecurities try to come in and make u feel otherwise, you should try crucifying your flesh.

Chapter Nineteen

Struggles

At some point in our lives we will all have to struggle with something. For some reason people think as soon as you become saved all the problems will end. But that's nowhere near the truth. As soon as you make that commitment to live your life for God the devil turns the fire on a little hotter. See, you're not a threat to the devil while you are living for him. No one will ever admit to living for Satan but your actions shows differently. If you party, smoke, drink, and fornicate, then my friend you are living for Satan. If your lifestyle doesn't reflect God, how can you say you love and live for him? Long as you are not contributing to the body of Christ you are fine and it gives the devil ample time to mess with Christians. One thing that I always tell people is the first time I really understood the significance of a struggle was when I became saved, and in my own opinion I feel as if that can go for everyone. You begin to get tested in every way you can think of. I understand some people's hardships growing up without a father, struggling to put food on the table, friends stabbing you in the back, and not being financially stable. But, when you come to Christ you will still have to go through trials like these, but the difference is that it's just a test that Satan gives to try and cripple you. When you have God on your side anything is possible.

Struggles come in all shapes and sizes. It doesn't matter if you are the preacher or the congregation, there's something we all are fighting to keep down. Just because a person is struggling in an area that does not mean they are a bad person or are living for the devil. Now, I'm not afraid to share my struggles with people because I know that it can help someone somewhere. I struggle with listening to hip hop music. I've tried almost every trick in the book to stop listening to secular music and it's hard. Does it mean that I'm not saved? No. Does it mean that I don't love God? No. Is it a weight? Yes. What I mean by saying that it's a weight is that it can potentially bring me down. It can form images and ideas in my head that can lead to other things. That's why I have to stay prayed up, and watch what I listen to. I'm not trying to justify any of the secular music, I already know it is all wrong but certain songs I try to avoid. I feel as if I have to start somewhere. If I hear a song that in the beginning rubs me the wrong way I won't listen to it. And then there are some artists who all together I don't listen to, no matter how popular they are. I pray every day for discernment because it's crucial that I'm aware of every position I put myself in.

I also struggle in another area, which I'm not proud of. I gossip a lot, I admit it. I try my best to keep my mouth shut but it is so hard. I never even knew that gossiping was a sin, and that God hated it. I have done it all my life and I even saw family members do it as well, so I never thought anything of it. One day I was listening to this Joel Osteen sermon and he was talking about these sins of the tongue that God hated, and gossiping was one of them. I have always been the type that's talking about something or someone, which is not profitable. I hate the fact that I'm like that so I try my best to watch what I say. It can be difficult at times because you have family members who gossip, coworkers that gossip, even social blogs that gossip. Everywhere you go people are partaking in this, making it harder. One scripture that I gravitate to for help is Proverbs 21:23 (ESV) which states, "He who guards his mouth and his tongue keeps himself from troubles." Sometimes when I'm at work I find myself in conversations I have no business being in, and I realize that it's another opportunity for the devil to work in me. At my job all that goes on is gossiping. I try my best to avoid it by going to the back, talking on the phone, or just going about my own business. But, then there are times when I fall for the trap and begin engaging in the conversation. A lot of the times I hear a voice saying, "Johnelle mind your own business and keep your mouth shut." I hear it a lot then I find myself all in someone else's business. When most of the conversations get to a certain point, I then realize that I have gone too far and I've dug myself a grave. A grave that's too deep to get out on my own. A line that I use a lot is, "Man, y'all got me gossiping." Truly I got myself gossiping and I lack self-control in that area. I'm aware that the tongue is a fire that's hard to put out. It's very challenging for me to not gossip but I'm getting better at it every day. I've seen the destruction that gossiping can do and I don't want any part of it.

Gossiping is deeper than you think, and one must be delivered. I cannot call myself a woman of God while gossiping about others. When you gossip you are basically reporting someone's sins to someone else. And the only person I know that has the right to judge is God. The scripture says in Proverbs 11:9 (KJV), "A hypocrite with his mouth destroyed his neighbor: but through knowledge shall the just be delivered." It's unacceptable to spread hearsay. With the time I'm using to gossip I could be spreading the word of God. Being a leader sometimes you have to be transparent and focus less on other people's problems, and reveal your struggles, because your struggles can help someone overcome theirs in due time.

Chapter Twenty*

Keep Your Eyes On
Your Paper

When you were growing up did you ever cheat off of someone else's paper because you thought they were smart, and then you get the results back and you failed? You then realized that you could have done better on your own. That's why it's important for us to keep our eyes on our own paper. Sometimes as Christians we find ourselves comparing our lives to other Christians. We should always be content with our portion. What God has for me, it is for me. We can't receive what God has for us if we are constantly looking at someone else's life. If God wanted you to have something he would make a way so you could have it. It does not mean that God doesn't love you because you are not driving a Benz like your neighbor. God sees everything and he knows what everyone can handle. Someone once asked me why God does not make sure every Christian is wealthy since the Bible talks about God having pleasure in our prosperity.

I had to break it down and let them know that God always wants what's best for us but everyone cannot handle it. Have you noticed how people act differently as soon as they get their income tax check? All it takes is a little bit of money and a person acts as if they have never been broke. A lot of times people will get large lump sums of money and stop going to church, paying their tithes, and the next thing you know their money becomes their idol. I think a lot of Christians stop trusting in God's plan and if something is not happening on their time they think that God does not want the best for them. If you fully trust God you will fully understand the purpose of your life and know that God will work everything out for your good. One phrase that I always use that I got from Joyce Meyer is that "when you complain you will remain". I don't think anyone wants to stay in the same situation because of dissatisfaction. I think we all may have had a time where we were not content with our situation.

Recently I was in a situation like this and I did not even know it until days later. I was meeting up with this guy I knew to chill. I went to his house and the first thing I noticed was that the neighborhood was very nice. When I walked in, he began telling me he owned the house. Now, I don't know too many twenty-five year olds who own their own home that's been built from the grown up at that. He gave me a tour of his home and it was beautiful. Nothing like what is in most young people houses and apartments I had seen. He began showing me his degrees and other ventures he was working on. I kept saying, "This is dope that you have your stuff together like this." I may have said that about ten times. I felt bad because I'm twenty-four years old, still live with my parents, working at a horrible fast food restaurant, making little-to-no pay. I do have a few ventures that I'm working on but none of them has taken off yet. That night I sat back and thought to myself that I needed to get myself together. I was beating myself up on the things I didn't have and was forgetting the things I do have such as an associate's degree, I work, I could be unemployed, and I'm working on a bachelor's degree. I was not even considering the fact that at that time I was rapping and in the process of writing this book. I began to think of a moment a while ago where one of my friends began to tell me, "You hang out with people in the same money bracket as you." Meaning that if you make six figures, then the people you associate yourself with will make six figures as well. If you work at a fast food restaurant the people you will surround yourself with will work at fast food restaurants as well. Now, I only agree with this statement to a point. I think it's all a mindset. If you're driven to accomplish something, you will, regardless on how the situation looks. I let all these things play a role into bringing me down. I couldn't believe for a split second I was coveting what someone had. I had to repent immediately because of my thinking. After all the scriptures I had in me, for one split second I forgot them all. Exodus 20:17 (ESV) states that, "You shall not covet your neighbor's house; you shall not covet your neighbor's wife, or his male servant, or his female servant, or his ox, or his donkey, or anything that's your neighbors."

I began to tell myself that I know that I will be successful in numerous ways (which I already knew from the beginning). But sometimes we can get distracted and forget the promise. As I think back on the situation I laugh because I'm positive that very soon I will own my own home, own a nice car, make a lot of money, and not only have ventures but change the world. Now I know this guy has no intentions of changing the world so I feel as if I'm already in the lead (even though this is not a competition). Now, if Satan tries another tactic to discourage me and get me to focus on another person's life I have experience. I just have to remember that the grass is not always greener on the other side. It may look appealing but only God knows what comes with their portion.

Chapter Twenty-One

Showing Love Through All Circumstances

As Christians, love should always be the goal. We should love everyone just as we love ourselves. Being that I'm young, often times I feel as if I can understand both worlds. I understand where the church comes from and what they represent. Then on the other hand you have the younger generation which no one seems to understand. I feel as if there is not enough love from the church going to the younger generation. It's like they have been written off for whatever reason. When people think of Christians they should get happy thoughts, but that's not always the case. Why is it that when people think of Christians they think of a bunch of hypocrites, fakes, phonies, and thieves? But why do they obtain this image? Somewhere along the way something occurred that made this younger generation think they would rather do bad than associate with Christians. Church is supposed to be a place where a person can come to be comforted. A lot of times when young people talk they speak on how they don't like religion but that they are spiritual. Even though their reasoning is misconstrued it's still somewhat of a fact to them.

I recently dealt with a situation where I felt as if a First Lady wasn't representing Christ as she should have. Before you guys start jumping to conclusions and think I'm judging her I'm going to break down the story for you. My friend and I were at this event because we were performing. It's something the community puts together every year called National Night Out. We didn't know what to expect when we got there so we tried to keep an open mind. We walked over to the location, and as soon as we got over I saw the pastor from the previous church me and my family used to attend on the microphone. I kept it moving and proceeded to walk to where my parents were. My friend and I began passing out some of our flyers to the people attending this event. When we walked around to the tent where the First Lady was we gave two of her members a flyer. Now, me and my friend were giving out two different flyers so we were taking turns on giving them out. My friend got to the First Lady first and she tried to hand her a flyer and she said, "We go to the same church", then she waved her off. Basically what she was saying was, "I don't want your flyer, if I want to look at it I will look at someone else's." Then I came up right after that and tried to give her my flyer and she told me the same thing, "We go to the same church."

Showing Love Through All Circumstances

Now, something with this picture is wrong. It's rare that you see young people doing something for God, and you always hear Christians talking about how they wish the younger generation would get saved and do something for Christ. So, what I'm trying to understand is that even if you do not care about what me and my friend are promoting, at least act like you care. It means a lot when you see Christians supporting other Christians. What I'm trying to get at is that when you are in a leadership position like that you should show love all the time because someone, somewhere is watching. I could have easily reacted differently and got smart with her or even asked her if she was saved, because she certainly was not acting like it. But, I smiled and kept it moving. I was taught to love everybody. There are people out here who have done me wrong, talked about me behind my back and I still treat them like it never happened. That's what a lot of Christians are lacking. No one cares about how many scriptures you can quote and how many members you have. If you are not showing love to people, all that stuff is irrelevant. People are always watching so it's best if you represent God well. I'm not trying to bash this lady or anything of that nature but people need to carry themselves accordingly when they are leaders. If this lady had a problem with my parents she should have solved it, given it to God, and smiled. Never take your anger out on anyone that doesn't deserve it. What if I didn't know better? What if I thought it was okay to treat people that way?

I grew up on love, so I know how it feels to be loved, and I know how to show it to others. I know how to smile when I should be frowning or fussing someone out. Some people do not know how to show love because they never experienced it for themselves. One thing that I catch myself telling people is to give everyone the benefit of the doubt. Even if you know the person is dead wrong, treat them with love. I refuse to let anyone steal my joy. I'm twenty-four and I understand that principle. I never let a person get to the point where they have that much control over me where they will steal my happiness. And it's always good to confuse that person as well as the enemy. People get confused when you smile and treat them nice after they done dragged your name in the dirt. Love is so much deeper than just telling someone you love them. John 13:34 states that we should love one another just as Christ loved us. I always have conversations with my friends about what my church would be like when I have one.

See, me and my friends embrace the fact that we are called to the ministry, and we occasionally talk about it. I'm known for saying, "When I get my church it's going to be different from anything you ever seen." I have seen a lot of things in church and since I'm young I notice what the youth gravitate to. And since the youth are in need of help more than ever before, I know I can do something. I just want to show the youth that I'm just like them and what proper leadership looks like and how leaders should show love no matter what the circumstances are. We all heard of the saying, "Actions speak louder than words," well that's what the world wants to see—being the living bible and showing everyone love in its purest form. The apostle Paul said that Christian love is the greatest and most essential of all the spiritual gifts. Even faith is worthless without love. We all must be aware that the church should be an example of what heaven will be like, so we should make an effort to abide in him and watch his love manifest in us. Showing love is always the start to something greater.

Chapter Twenty-Two

Step Into Your Calling

We all have a calling that we need to step into. The question is who will be obedient to God's voice. I know a lot of people, especially my age, who think that they have time but, time is of the essence. God has so much in store for us and all he wants us to do is step out and get it. But first you have to be in God's will. God doesn't care about your past; he cares about your NOW. Your past does not disqualify you from his blessings. Just imagine how many souls you can save if you answer God's call. I know a lot of you may be wondering, "What is my calling?" Everyone can't hear from God. So, how can you be sure what area God is calling you in? Everyone's calling is not to be a preacher, singer, or some public figure. Some people's calling are to do things behind the scenes, and those roles are just as important as a preacher. If you are in a position right now and you are trying to find out what your calling is check your motives. Next time a leader asks you to clean up the church, stay later, or drive the church van, DO IT! And work it as if you were a preacher. God loves to see how you deal with small things, to see if you are capable of handling bigger ones. When I first got saved I was so anxious and excited I wanted to put my hands in everything. You name it; I was trying to do it. I knew that when I met God at the throne he was going to want to know if I stepped into my calling and used the gifts he gave me. God doesn't give you gifts for no reason. God gives you gifts to be a blessing to other people. I never knew that I would be rapping, doing poetry, writing a book, and making YouTube videos, it's like it all came together one by one. Now, what if I didn't step out and started rapping, I wouldn't even have tried to do poetry. God knows how to set you up for the right things in his perfect timing.

One thing that I believe that a person who has a calling on their life needs to want is an overflow. By overflow I mean a divine anointing. An excessive amount of God's Holy Spirit. You can get an overflow in numerous ways, such as wisdom, vision, and success. The list goes on. Being drenched in favor and abundance is by far the best feeling. I used to pray to God to fill my cup (same thing as asking for an overflow) but, at the time I really did not know what I was asking for. I received it and I felt as if I was pleasing God when I took that initiative. It felt as if I put my foot down and told the devil I would no longer be a slave to him but rather step into God's calling on my life. Matthew 5:6 (NIV) says, "Blessed are those who hunger and thirst for righteousness, for they shall be filled." The closer you draw to Christ the closer he will draw near to you. It's okay to ask God for a little help. To be quite frank, we can't do this thing called life on our own.

Maybe you are scared to step into your calling. Maybe you are scared to ask for an overflow. Maybe you are scared to ask for help. You should cast down those thoughts immediately because it's a trick of the devil who is trying to prevent you from doing God's will. Nothing makes the devil angrier than stepping into your calling. He's totally fine with you going to church, singing in the choir, even paying your little tithes. But as soon as you do what's pleasing unto God the devil is in fear. We all say we love God and we will do anything for him, now here's your chance to do so. What is holding you back from stepping into your calling? That party next week, your boyfriend/girlfriend, your job, your friends? Well, while these material things are holding you back, these material things you cannot take with you when you die. So choose, but choose wisely. The bible states in Matthew 6:19 (NLT), "Do not store up treasures here on earth, where moths eat them and rust destroys them, and where thieves break in and steal." Our objective should be focused on heavenly things. A scripture that gets me every time and makes me want to do right is Romans 8:34 (NLT). It states, "Who then will condemn us? No one—for Christ Jesus died for us and was raised to life for us, and he is sitting in the place of honor at God's right hand, pleading for us." It blows my mind that Jesus loves us that much that he's in heaven interceding on our behalf because he has faith that we will get it right.

There are so many things that we need to put into perspective but we don't. Stepping into your calling is not something you should do as a last resort, it should be a priority. How many drug dealers, crack heads, prostitutes, and rebellious children do you know? We all can be the light to someone that's falling into darkness. I have that much respect for God that I will put my pride to the side and try to make a difference. Many of us do not have that push to step out, but as long as you have Jesus interceding for you that's all that should matter.

Chapter Twenty-Three

You Can't Save Everybody

Something that I had to learn the hard way was that not everyone wants to live for Christ. Some people are happy with the way their life is going. What people fail to realize is that living in sin is fun. It's sad but it's true. There are not any rules to follow; you can live your life however you want. The Bible talks about Satan being the prince of the air, which simply means that God has given Satan power over the world. He can influence the world in a way where living in darkness is appealing and appears to be better than being saved. To this day I ask myself why so many people have a messed up mindset about God, and I have yet to find an answer. Everyone that knows me knows that I'm always trying to save someone. I have stories for days about times I bent over backwards to get someone to come to Christ. I was once listening to a T.D Jakes sermon and he said, "You never experienced hurt until you tried to help someone that refused it." For some reason I have an idea in my head that I'm capable of helping everyone. There are just some people out there that if God himself came down to help them they still wouldn't change. The sad part that I don't understand is how saved people can have this mindset at times. They grow up in the church, feel the Holy Spirit, speak in tongues, the whole nine yards and still conform to the way of the world. Those people are the ones that I feel sorry for the most because they know better, but prefer living their lives pleasing to their flesh.

The other day I was in the barbershop with my friend and there was this guy inside the shop talking about how there is no God. He was very loud, as if he was talking to the entire shop, but he was only talking to three people. He was going on about what type of person creates people and allows bad things to happen to them. I honestly don't have the answer to any of these questions but my God does. And everything will be revealed to us in due time. But for this guy, he chooses to be ignorant, and there are plenty of people on Earth like him. Those people don't want to understand, they just want to be a rebel and cause confusion. God does not like confusion, and he does not operate in that order. Some people are going straight to hell and there is nothing anyone can do about it. No matter how many times a person goes to church, sing in the choir, or pray, we have to face the fact that if a person wants God wholeheartedly they will seek after him so they can escape eternal damnation. I came to the conclusion that I need to worry about myself. I should not put all my time and effort in trying to save someone because I have my own struggles I'm trying to overcome. It's unfortunate that some people are lost but all we can do is pray.

An important scripture that I would like to relay to unbelievers is that in Philippians 2:10 (NIV) states that, "that at the name of Jesus every knee should bow, in heaven and on earth and under the earth." You can think God is fake or evil all you want but when you meet him face to face you have no choice but to respect him. It's better that we get our lives right while we are on this earth, because after we leave here we will start something somewhere else. Maybe you are a person that believes in God but don't truly seek after him as you should. You should pray for strength because unbelievers are the devil's handy work and whatever they do or say it's to poison you. You can't be weak and expect to win a battle set up by the enemy. God wants more of us and all we have to do is develop a relationship with him. Just remember that the war is not with flesh and blood but with evil rulers and authorities of the unseen world. So, make up your mind today and try to be the best example you can be for unbelievers as well as believers. And when all else fails, you should pray because everyone does not want Christ as bad as you do.

Chapter Twenty-Four

Transformational Thinking

There is a time in this walk when you have to be transformed. It's impossible to be the same person you were in the beginning of your walk. The Bible states in 2 Corinthians 5:17: Therefore, that if anyone is in Christ, he is a new creation. The old has passed away; behold, the new has come." With that being said, you have to be changed internal as well as external. Being transformed is not something that can be accomplished in a day. Transformation is a process and it's something we all battle with daily. We have to continue to remind ourselves that the transformation process is not something that you can do one time and you're good. Let me break down to you what transformation really means. It means to change. That the renewal of the mind from the previous lifestyle, the carnal mind, no longer conforms to the ways of this world. You have to begin the transformation process spiritually. Feeding your spirit constantly is the key, and people will eventually see the results on the outside.

Transformation is a long process and something you have to continue to work on. Every day I see myself getting better at transformational thinking. There were a lot of things that I needed to change that I did not even know was a problem. As I look back on my life I thank God on how far I have gotten, but I still have more to tackle. I never really knew how bad my thinking was until recently.

I was in church one Sunday and one of the youth was speaking and she decided to do a "no negative" fast to prepare for her sermon. I took her idea and ran with it and I decided to do a no negative fast as well. With the fast I made sure I didn't do anything negative. So, I tried my best to speak positive things, and even think positive things as well. This was the hardest thing I ever did. I never knew how messed up my thinking was until the fast. My mindset was disgusting. I was critical of people, judgmental, and a huge gossiper. You name it, I was living that way in my mind. Second Corinthians 10:5 (KJV) tells us to "[Cast] down imaginations, and every high thing that exalted itself against the knowledge of God, and bringing into captivity every thought to the obedience of Christ." That fast helped me realize that I have a lot more work to do with myself. Now, this was the start of me recognizing how bad I needed to transform my mind, I would not have even noticed because I read the bible, go to church, pray and worship. But sometimes you have to dig a little deeper.

Everyone that knows me knows that the person I am now is totally different from who I used to be. It used to be to the point where I did not care what I said out of my mouth—and I WAS a CHRISTIAN. I simply did not fully understand what it meant to be transformed. That's why it is very important to keep learning. There is always something new to learn. Sometimes I'm amazed at how my thinking has done a complete 180. I'm not perfect but, I'm trying my best to achieve greatness.

A few things that stand out about the old me is that I used to say I never wanted kids and I never want to be married. I do not even know why I even felt like that. My thinking was so messed up and I thought it was cool. Most young girl's dreams are to get married and have a family, but I was beyond reckless with my mindset. Probably around a year ago I decided that I wanted to get married and have kids. It was like pulling teeth to get me to come to that conclusion. But I can't just pick and choose what parts of the Bible I want to live by. It does not work like that. We have to live 100% for God. And it's even worse to know what the Bible says to do and then do the complete opposite. I want to do what is pleasing to God. The Bible speaks on God wanting his children to be fruitful and multiply. How can we do that with an attitude of "I don't want any kids nor marriage?" There was a time where I would never read anything pertaining to marriage or children because it just "wasn't me." Now, I find myself reading blogs, books, and sermons about marriage and children. This is where the transformation in my thinking comes about. I had to stop the fleshly thinking and educate myself and refuse to give my flesh what it wanted. To be honest, I was just being ignorant. I had to put away childish things and that was the beginning for me.

Sad to say, this was not the only example where I had to change my way of thinking. One day I was at work and me and the coworkers were having a discussion that was very juicy. I brought it up, and I asked everyone if it was the night of their bachelorette/bachelor party would they let their fiancé cheat on them. Everyone said, "Yes," except for about two people. This topic was ongoing for about three days and everyone had something to say about it. Then they asked me what I would do and I said, "Yes, it's best if he get it out of his system since he's going to be a dead man walking."

I didn't think anything was wrong with it and I didn't see what the big deal was. Then we asked my older manager and her boyfriend their opinion. They gave me a different perspective on the topic. What if someone gets pregnant, or someone catches feelings or even wants to do it again? Then they added, "Aren't you a Christian?" I began to laugh because I honestly forgot that I was literally holding conversations from a carnal mind. Now, what made me even think like this? It was the fact that my thinking was not transformed. I spoke of things that I was thinking about. Somewhere I let something in, and I did not even realize it. I thought to myself, "I got so much to learn and work on." A person who is on fire for God easily let something slip in. This is a perfect example that shows me and other people that no matter what level you are on you will still have to transform your thinking. If we do not continue to put the word in us and work on ourselves daily, something can enter us and change the way we look at things as well as how we think, and we would never know.

It may seem as if transformation thinking is hard but, it is only hard if you do not try. Your mind and heart are very important with this walk and they have great control over our lives. Would you prefer to walk around with a polluted mind and heart? The Bible says in Matthew 15:18 that the words you speak come from the heart, that's what defiles you. Every day since that day I think about what I am thinking about because I do not ever want to say something that will confuse the people I am preaching to. I do not want to feel as if I'm living a double life, and certain sinful things are okay when they're not.

In Conclusion

My purpose and goal for this book is to touch many people's lives. I know I may not have all the answers and I may not have "Reverend" in front of my name but, I'm qualified. I took the initiative to write this book and follow God's directions step-by-step, and believe me it wasn't easy. When I got finished with this book and I realized how many pages I had I was devastated. I immediately started calling people complaining about how it wasn't enough, and this isn't a "real book," people are going to take me as an amateur. Everything that I learned and everything I tried to teach people with this book, I forgot about it that quick. I felt like this book was supposed to be a blessing, and just as quickly I felt as if it was a curse.

A lot of times we easily offer the devil the game. We let him win the battle without even a fight. I want to be a fighter because I know that I am more than a conqueror. What I'm trying to get you to understand is that everything we go through in life is a STORY and God gives all of us a story to share with people. Our stories are our gifts. To be a blessing to people we have to share gifts with them. In no way, shape, or form am I trying to brag about anything throughout this book. All I want to do is share a few things with people and pray that my mess can be a message to someone and help them grow.

We all are fighting with something. It doesn't matter what age, ethnicity you are, or background you have, we all will still be fighting with something. But that's not an excuse to give up. God will not feel sorry for you because you have a fight. I'm fighting with something as you read this. I'm dealing with health issues, I have a tumor (mass) in my liver that the doctors are watching for it to shrink so that it will not turn into cancer. I could have easily written a whole chapter about that seeking for attention and a pity party, but I didn't. That's not the purpose of this book. I don't like dealing with it but, I know it may not feel good TO ME, but I know that it's good FOR ME. That's why I named this book "Fighting to be what God has longed for me to be" because we all are fighting for something that will eventually transform us into the person God wants.

My prayer is for everyone who takes their time in reading my book and understanding where I'm coming from to see that I'm doing everything out of love. I can be sarcastic and use my dry sense of humor at times but please do not take offense at anything I say. I want the best for everyone, and I'm looking forward to seeing my people in Heaven someday. One love.....

About the Author

Johnelle Johnson was born in a small city in Chesapeake, Virginia, on March 9, 1990. She is a disciple of Jesus Christ ministering to youth in a way attractive to the younger generation. She is a member of Faith in Action Church in Norfolk, Virginia. She is also a member of a gospel rap group by the name of Street Ministry. She does poetry in her free time, as well as short video blogs, and enjoys photography.

Johnelle also has an Associate's Degree in Business Administration. She's attending Old Dominion University pursuing a Bachelor's Degree in Mass Communication, and will graduate in May 2015. Johnelle has as a goal, alongside with her group member Cetra, to make Street Ministry a bigger movement so youth can come together and change the world as we know it. Today Johnelle lives in Suffolk, Virginia, preaching the gospel on a regular basis to employees, family and friends, while continuing to rap for the glory of God.

www.ingramcontent.com/pod-product-compliance
Lightning Source LLC
LaVergne TN
LVHW051648080426
835511LV00016B/2557